TAKE IT FROM HERE

Program Resources for Women

Compiled by Evelyn Stenbock

All you need to know to plan a rich, exciting calendar of events for the women's group in your church!

Contents

Installation Ideas
  If the Shoe Fits, Wear It—by Irene B. Brand   2
  Keys—by Gean D. Smith   5
  Certain Women—by Dorothy Hughes   6

Poetry and Readings   8

Monthly Program Material
  School Days—by Evelyn Stenbock   16
  Another Year—by Ethel V. Leffel   20
  On the Subject of Hearts—by Ethel V. Leffel   21
  King of Glory Easter Program—by Carolyn R. Scheidies   23
  I Am a Woman—by Gean D. Smith   Inside Back Cover
  The Covered Dish Convention—by Gail Blanton   24

A One-Act Play for Three Women
  Del's Woodsman—by Ted Scoggins   27

Mother's Day Banquet
  A Hawaiian Evening—by Helen Kitchell Evans   34

Permission to make photocopies of this book is granted to the purchaser when three copies have been purchased. These copies cannot be sold, loaned, or given away.

Copyright © 1981 by Lillenas Publishing Co.
All Rights Reserved.   Litho in U.S.A.

Lillenas Publishing Co.
KANSAS CITY, MO. 64141

Installation Ideas

If the Shoe Fits, Wear It

(An installation service for women's groups)

By Irene B. Brand

Preparation—
1. For advance publicity, cut a large shoe from poster board, recording the time and date of the meeting, and other pertinent information.
2. Cut medium-sized shoe from construction paper for each officer to be installed, listing the duties of an officer on each shoe. Example: Duties of the President—I will serve as presiding officer at the meetings.
3. Have smaller shoes, with pledges of support written on them, for each person attending the meeting. Example: I will pray for the president.

Other suggested pledges:
—I will faithfully attend the society meetings.
—I will pray for our missionaries.
—I will contribute to the missionary quota of the church.

SUGGESTED SCRIPTURES—
—Ephesians 6:15
—Proverbs 4:26
—Proverbs 3:23
—John 8:12
—1 Thessalonians 4:12

Song—"O Master, Let Me Walk with Thee"

Opening Meditation *(by the person who installs the officers)*—

Most of us may have said, at one time or another, "If I were in her shoes, I would . . ." Such a statement is easy to make, but in all probability, if we were wearing the shoes of the people we're judging, we would duplicate their actions. The Indian's prayer is good advice for us, "Great Spirit, grant that I may not criticize my neighbor until I have walked a mile in his moccasins."

When we consider the pathways followed by many great leaders, both past and present, we realize that it would have been difficult to wear their shoes. In this service, we will cite examples of Christian women leaders to encourage us to accept the work to be done in our society.

PART I—Could we have worn the shoes of the following women of the past . . . ?

RUTH, the Moabitess, who forsook her family, her homeland, and her god, to follow Naomi to a strange country. Because Ruth accepted the God of the Hebrews, she was used as a vessel to transmit David's royal blood to Jesus.

HANNAH, whose longing for a son was satisfied with the ordained birth of Samuel. Once the child was a reality, could we, like Hannah, have kept our vow and delivered Samuel to the Temple?

MARY, the mother of Jesus, whose virtuous life made her suitable for God's divine purpose. But, could we have followed her footsteps to the Cross, to watch in sorrow the crucifixion of her beloved Son?

ANNE HUTCHINSON, resident of Massachusetts in the 1600s who dared to criticize the doctrine of the leaders of Massachusetts Bay Colony. Because she taught her neighbors to follow freedom of conscience in their worship of God, she was banished from the colony. She, and her family, were later massacred by Indians in New York.

NARCISSA WHITMAN, one of the first white women to cross the Rocky Mountains. She shared her missionary husband's zeal to take the gospel to the Northwest Indians. Narcissa and her husband were also killed by the Indians.

DOROTHEA DIX, the Massachusetts woman who dedicated her life and used her fortune to improve conditions for the insane throughout the United States and abroad.

PART II—Could we wear the shoes of present-day spiritual leaders? (*In this part of the program, each local society should cite the names and work of missionaries or other leaders who have made significant contributions to the work of their denomination.*)

PART III—**The Installation Service** (*Prospective officers will all stand before the installing leader.*)

LEADER (*to president*)—
   Your function is to lead in planning and carrying through a program which will involve all church women. Will you accept this shoe?
   (*She hands the candidate for president, a "shoe" with duties of the office written on it. The same procedure will be followed by the rest of the officers.*)

PRESIDENT (*reading*)—Yes, I will:
—serve as presiding officer at the meetings, and be an ex officio member of all committees.
—give leadership in formulating and implementing plans to help carry out the purpose of the organization.
—attend, and encourage attendance, at local, state, and national meetings.
—study and follow rules of parliamentary procedure.
—involve as many women as possible in the work of the organization.
—meet annually with officers and chairwomen to evaluate the year's work.

GROUP *(speaks in unison after each officer reads her duties)*—
   If the shoe fits, wear it.

LEADER *(to vice-president)*—
   Your duty is to inspire women to positive action in the mission of the church through programming and to guide in planning the total program for the year. Will you wear this shoe?

VICE-PRESIDENT *(reading)*—Yes, I will:
—serve as an assistant to the president and preside at the meetings in her absence.
—plan programs.
—become familiar with the purposes of the organization, and endeavor to incorporate those purposes into the programs.

GROUP—If the shoe fits, wear it.

LEADER *(to secretary)*—
   As secretary, you should keep accurate minutes of all meetings, and publicize and promote the program and activities of the group. Will you accept this responsibility?

SECRETARY *(reading)*—Yes, I will:
—try to attend all meetings and keep a correct record of the organization's activities.
—handle all correspondence promptly.
—serve as liaison between the organization and church publications, as well as local newspapers.

GROUP—If the shoe fits, wear it.

LEADER *(to treasurer)*—
   Will you render suitable stewardship of all funds accumulated by the organization?

TREASURER *(reading)*—Yes, I will:
—keep an accurate account of all money entrusted to the group, and make a financial report at each meeting.
—pay all obligations and pledges promptly.
—consider myself a steward owing my responsibility to God, as well as to the organization.

GROUP—If the shoe fits, wear it.

LEADER *(to devotional chairman)*—
   In this office, you should motivate each woman toward a deeper spiritual life. How do you respond?

DEVOTIONAL CHAIRMAN—I will:
—strengthen my own personal prayer, study, and meditation.
—encourage members to engage in private and family devotions.
—promote regular church attendance and participation in the total church program.

GROUP—If the shoe fits, wear it.
   (If the women's group has more officers to install, this basic plan can be followed, and appropriate officers and their duties added.)

PART IV—Dedication of the Members
(Individual members stand and read the pledges from their "shoes.")
(In closing, all repeat the following verse, in unison.)

> We will wear these shoes with humility
> As along sacred ways we walk;
> For God's work leads to paths most holy,
> And calls for service, not just talk.

PRAYER OF DEDICATION by the leader.

Keys

An Installation Service

By Gean D. Smith

Equipment—Four keys of various sizes will be needed. The large one should be very large; the smallest one tiny. Wooden keys can be made and painted with gold or silver spray paint. As each key is presented, the candidate repeats the following vows.

Chairman—This large key informs me that my work is a large and important one. This organization's success will largely rest upon me and my willingness to dedicate myself to this good work.

Secretary/Treasurer—My key is the key of organization and financial stability. Unless I use my key properly, this organization will be confused in its records and its financial standing.

Program Chairman—My key is the key of music and program material. I intend to bring sweet music to our meetings and keep us singing throughout the year.

Social Chairman—This tiny key does not mean that my office is insignificant or small. This key will open up the doors of fellowship, so I hold the key to failure or success of our organization!

Dedicatory Pledge *(in unison)*—We pledge to use our keys to bring peace and harmony to our organization. We pledge this year to be a year of singing and fellowship, as well as service.

Prayer *(led by president or chairman)*—Lord, help us to seek and do Your will as we attempt to lead this organization in the year ahead. Help us to turn to You for guidance and strength.

Certain Women

An Installation Service

By Dorothy Hughes

Hymn—"Stand Up, Stand Up for Jesus"

Scripture Reading—Luke 8:1-3

(Leaders stand across front, facing members. Each steps forward as her name is called.)

Installing Officer—We have come to recognize the leaders of _____
(organization)
_____ who have been elected and have agreed to serve during 19___. I wish to give each of you newly elected leaders two things:

1. A phrase, taken from the words of "Stand Up, Stand Up for Jesus."
2. An example, taken from stories of women in the Bible.

To you, our _____, _____,
(office)   (name)
I give the phrase "Lift high His royal banner."
I give you the example of Deborah, the Jeanne d'Arc of Israel. Deborah saw what God wanted to be done and inspired the people to follow her in doing it. Her battle cry was "Up, for this is the day in which the Lord hath delivered . . ."
When the battle had been won, Deborah led in praise to the Lord. We look to you, our _____, to lift high His royal banner and inspire
(office)
us toward victories in the work of _____.
(organization)

To you, our _____, and _____, I give the
(office)   (name)
phrase "Now serve Him." I find in the listing of your duties the recurring obligation to serve as appointed.

I give you the example of Phoebe, a woman who could be trusted to fulfill her obligations. The apostle Paul trusted her to deliver his precious letter to the Christians in Rome. The two verses of Scripture which tell all we know about Phoebe, describe her with three words: *servant, saint, succourer.*

A life of self-giving through many kindnesses and much service to others is hidden away under those words. As you fulfill your appointments this year, you will find occasions to serve Him as servant, saint, and succourer.

To you, our _____, _____, I give the phrase
(office)   (name)
"next the victor's song."

I give you the example of Miriam, chosen and qualified by the Lord to assist in the redemption of His people. Miriam had the spirit within her which caused people to follow. On that glorious day when God led His people through the Red Sea to freedom, it was Miriam who led them in an anthem of rejoicing. When we gather again a year from now to review those things you have recorded, may they be a victor's song!

To you, our _____ (office), _____ (name), I give the phrase "Christ is Lord, indeed."

I give you the example of Lydia, known in the Bible as a generous woman.

She was successful in business and gave to the work of Christ both her means and her influence. I also give you the example of the widow whose offering of two mites was praised by Jesus. Jesus noted her sacrifice and love for God when she gave all she had.

You, as _____ (office), will encourage others to give as these did, in the consciousness that Christ is Lord of every part of our lives.

To you, our _____ (office), _____ (name), I give the phrase "let courage rise with danger."

I give you the example of Abigail, a woman the Bible describes as "of good understanding." She saw a difficult situation, then used her intelligence and good judgment to settle it peacefully.

We look to you to guide our course of action with the courage born of good understanding.

To you, our _____ (office), _____ (name), I give the phrase "where duty calls."

I give you the example of Priscilla, whose duties led her to Corinth, Ephesus, Rome. Wherever we find Priscilla, her home and heart are open to serve the Lord.

Priscilla was not a casual church worker, she became deeply involved. She could lead without offending others or displaying herself. Your duty will call you to attend meetings, to promote plans and programs. May you look upon this call of duty, not as an obligation to be fulfilled, but as a joyful service to be rendered.

(Ask all members to stand.)

To you, all members of _____ (organization), I give the phrase "His army shall He lead." This is a promise, "His army *shall* He lead, till ev'ry foe is vanquished and Christ is Lord, indeed."

I give you the question asked of Esther: "Who knoweth whether thou art come to the kingdom for such a time as this?" The question challenges us, as it did Esther. You, with all your potential of prayer, gifts, and service, are needed for such a time as this. The work of _____ (organization) depends not only on these leaders but on every member. Let us leaders and members together follow the examples of these certain Bible women in the promotion of _____ (purpose of organization: service, missions, Bible study) during 19____.

Prayer of Dedication

Poetry and Readings

Hold On to the Rope

When trials of life surround you,
   Hold on to the rope, my friend.
God is with you, pulling for you;
   He's on the other end!

The days seem dark and cloudy,
   Family problems that just won't mend.
Hold on to the rope and you'll come through
   With God on the other end.

At night the sleep just will not come;
   Hold on 'til the morning, and then
The day will brighten your troubles,
   For God's on the other end!

—*Helen Kitchell Evans*

"Home Mission"

She also serves whose home-bound spirit gives
   A cup of water in the Savior's name.
Who, in the shadows, quiet, humble, lives
   To bring the Master glory and acclaim.

A barley loaf—and fishes—small indeed
   In her small hand. But with His hand to bless,
Enough to feed a hungry multitude
   On Living Bread, and love, and selflessness.

How beautiful the feet whose dusty steps
   Glad tidings bring to peoples still unblessed!
As beautiful the hand of her who bathes
   The dust, and gives the footsore traveler rest.

A warrior still is she whose battlefield
   The smallest place of prayer, unknown, unsung.
Not small the God who holds the warrior's shield,
   Not small the Savior's answer, "Child, well done!"

—*Ethel V. Leffel*

Take Heart and Try Again

If you should find that you have failed
And that no good have you availed,
Though ills your progress have assailed
    And all for you seems vain,
Just bundle up your doubts and fears,
Then toss them out and give three cheers!
Say to yourself, in spite of jeers,
    That you will try again.

What you can't do the good Lord can;
There's nothing can His power ban,
So try once more the race you ran,
    With prayer deep in your soul.
Trust in the strength of His own might
And He will always lead aright.
Take heart again with hope that's bright,
    And you will reach your goal!
                  —*Vida Munden Nixon*

I'll Keep on Singing!

If the roses stop their blooming
    And the birds refuse to sing,
And the oceans cease their roaring
    And the bells refuse to ring,
If the nations all shall tumble
    And the babies never smile,
And the preachers all stop preaching
    I will trust Him all the while!
I will keep on singing, singing,
    For I know I'm not alone.
For my Jesus loves and keeps me,
    And God still is on His throne!
               —*Gean D. Smith*

The God of Years

God is the God of years—
God of happiness and blinding tears.
He is the God of all eternity and time,
Who He, himself alone,
Gives life its reason and its rhyme!
               —*Ethel V. Leffel*

In Jesus

There is a joy in Jesus
    that sees beyond the knarled,
    dog-eared corners of pages
    and precepts.
There is a hope in Jesus—
    not that spring always
    follows winter, but that
    it will one day begin
    and never end.
There is a peace in Jesus—
    deeper, wider, calmer
    than the structured order
    of His Universe unfolding!
There is a faith in Jesus
    that He never changes,
    that He cannot lie,
    nor fail, nor forsake.
There is a love in Jesus
    greater than knowledge,
    and wisdom—above
    understanding—
    and so infinitely real!
               —*Jim Gibbs*

"From Whence Cometh My Strength?"

I reached my hand bravely into the New Year,
But in the strife of wars of years gone past
I didn't think I'd find much joy or peace.
With troubles in the world,
And in our homes, the bulwark of our land,
My courage wasn't real—
But like the little boy's who whistled
As he passed the cemetery in the dark.

And then I heard a voice—
The voice of God:
"Be not afraid. I'm with you every day.
I needn't stretch My hand at all
To feel the way, nor whistle in the dark!"

And like a spark, my heart was lifted.
For God, who said to David,
"I'm your strength,"
Is still the God today—my God.
He leads the way!

—Ethel V. Leffel

Have You?

Have you ever seen a trusting baby's smile,
Or stood protective over helpless newborn things,
Or watched red cardinals walk on diamonds in the snow,
Realizing the earth was preparing for the birth of spring?
Have you stood at dawn and watched the rising sun
Paint amazing combinations across the canvas sky,
Or gazed upon the same procedure at eventide,
'Til darkness fell, and stars began to twinkle there on high?
Have you stood in the moonlight and listened intently
As the noises of the night creatures slowly increased,
Or heard the pitter patter of the raindrops on the lawn,
And felt the tension of your body replaced with peace?
Have you ever seen a pain-filled body allowed to rest
When a crisis was reached and passed and hope awakened,
Or given up a loved one to the one way gate to death,
And felt alone and small, helpless, and forsaken?
Have you ever seen the earth crack, and rivers rise and fall,
Or heard the wind softly murmur, or heard its angry squall,
Or seen the lightning flash, and heard the thunder roll,
Or heard the breakers dashing against the ocean wall?
If you have seen these you have shaken hands with God,
You have seen His gentle smile and heard Him say, "Remember."
Oh, what eternal joy is yours if you humbly surrendered!
Oh, what a loss if you met Him, and left Him, still a stranger!

—Mattie Ridgeway

God's Little Creatures

Cute little creatures are wonderful teachers;
God in the heavens had purpose for all;
Ants are all working, crickets all chirping,
Birds nest their babies in treetops so tall!
Down in the earth and high up in the sky
They are too busy to even ask why
People are lazy—like such folks as I!

—*Vida Munden Nixon*

The Glory of God

Did you ever see a soul in deep despair?
Wallow in the depths of sin and didn't care?
Then to see a hand reach down
And lift him from the fallen ground—
   Oh, a soul that's turned to Jesus
   Is the glory of the Lord!

Did you ever walk alone through shadows deep?
Were you burdened in the night and couldn't sleep?
Then you heard a thrilling Word
Of the sweetest story ever heard—
   Oh, the soul that turns to Jesus
   Is the glory of the Lord!

—*Gean D. Smith*

What Could One Expect?

Two fresh eggs, sugar, butter, and flour,
   A mental image of a magazine cover cake,
I carefully mix and set the heat control,
   I follow every step the recipe relates.
Beating 1 minute, then 2 minutes more,
   Then pouring into the size of pan it takes,
Only 35 minutes in the oven, no more,
   Just time to make the icing while it slowly bakes.

The doorbell rings under a neighbor's hand,
   And I rush to answer for friendship's sake.
She has been to town and heard the news.
   I sit spellbound, she breathlessly prates.
"Have you heard about the mayor's daughter,
   And the only son of the Widow Spakes?"
Attention wanders 'til the sense of smell reminds me.
   In my oven now are two crisply burned flakes.

—*Mattie Ridgeway*

Harvest

I planted the seeds and watched them grow
   And tended them carefully.
Some came up strong and some seemed weak
   But I hoed them hopefully.

All summer long they grew and grew
   And the work I did seemed good.
For most of them survived and gave
   Good food, like I hoped they would.

My baskets are full with love and food
   For in life I did no guessing.
And "as I sowed so have I reaped"
   I'm receiving a bountiful blessing.

        —*Dorothy Delaney Roberts*

The Flower—Love

The most prized flower known in all the world
   Is not the one that's watched o'er carefully,
When all its leaves and petals are dew pearled,
   And, perfect, wins the prize so truthfully.

The most prized flower in all the world
   Is planted, but is planted all unknown,
It grows and grows until it is unfurled
   In all its beauty, then it is full grown.

It's kindness, planted in the hearts of all
   That is the seed which grows to sun above,
And fed on trust and mercy bursts its shawl,
   And blossoms soon into a flower—love.

        —*Mattie Ridgeway*

Face-to-Face

When this life is over and I've run this earthly race,
All I really long to see is Jesus, face-to-face!
I look not for mansions, nor long for leisure pace—
All I really long to see is Jesus, face-to-face!
I'll end my earthly travel and by my Savior's grace,
I'll see what I have longed to see—Jesus, face-to-face!

        —*Gean D. Smith*

Shadows

Shadows flickering on a wall,
Making things seem very tall.
I close my eyes and hide my head,
Shivering and shaking in my bed.
Dear Jesus, sweet Jesus, come be with me!
I'm so afraid of the dark, You see!
After some moments the peace does come,
I feel the presence of the Mighty One.
With new courage I lift my head,
Throw back the covers and jump out of bed.
I run to the window, pick up the shade;
Gaze at the night where shadows are made.
The moon and the stars shine down on my face,
My heart now beats at a normal pace.
My soul sings out in silent praise;
Sweet Jesus, dear Jesus, my fears are erased!

—*Janet A. Rock*

Happiness Is Jesus

Happiness is Jesus
  While on this earth below,
Happiness is Jesus
  As on life's path you go.
Just take it all to Jesus
  When friends are sometimes few,
And rest upon His promise—
  He'll surely see you through.

When shadows overwhelm you
  And you feel so all alone,
Just lift your eyes toward heaven—
  He'll give your heart a song.
He'll plant your feet on solid ground
  And give you life anew,
For happiness is Jesus,
  He loves and cares for you!

—*Helen C. Wyrick*

The Sweetest Story

I don't live in a fancy mansion,
  And I haven't any gold,
But I possess a story—
  The sweetest ever told.

It's all about my Jesus
  Who died on Calvary.
I know the sweetest story,
  And that's good enough for me.

I haven't any treasure,
  Let me state before I start.
The story's in the Bible,
  And His love is in my heart.

For the day that I met Jesus
  He said He'd set me free.
I'll live with Him in glory—
  That's good enough for me!

—*Gean D. Smith*

Trusting in Jesus

I'm trusting in Jesus wherever I go;
I'll follow His footsteps on earth here below.
Wherever I wander on life's stormy sea,
I'm trusting in Jesus—His hand's guiding me.

I'm trusting in Jesus, my Savior above.
I'm trusting in Jesus and His infinite love.
Wherever I wander on life's stormy sea,
I'm trusting in Jesus—His hand's guiding me.

If you need a refuge from sorrow and care,
Run quickly to Jesus—your burden He'll bear;
He'll give peace and comfort, He'll free you from sin—
Just trusting in Jesus new life will begin!

—*Helen C. Wyrick*

Find Someone in Need

Find some weary person
  Alone and in the dark;
Try to cheer their spirit
  By lending them a spark.
Give them hope by showing
  A glimmer of love's light,
And soon they will be knowing
  A pathway that is bright.

—*Vida Munden Nixon*

Spring

I love the spring
The dear old spring,
  That brings the pretty flowers.
I love the trees,
With bright green leaves,
  That shine in April showers.

When frost will leave,
And winds blow free,
  Then spring is really here,
With sunshine bright,
And birds in flight
  Who tell us summer's near.

—*Mattie Ridgeway*

Who?

Who has time to question snow
Or wonder why the rivers flow—
Or meditate on sand and sea
Or why the sky bounds endlessly?

And who has never pondered death
Or felt the winds withdrawing breath?
And who has never marveled sight
Or gloried at the day and night?

And who can comprehend how thought
And minds and knowledge all were wrought?
And who can say if dreams are true,
And who is wise, and what are you?

And who can say they'll ever know
Why we are here and where we'll go
In a universe of stars and night,
Of souls and suns, of wrong and right?

And who has skill to understand
How it all was made by God's great hand?
For all that is, both great and small,
Christ is He who made it all!

—*Jim Gibbs*

The Weaver

The loom is ready,
    The warp all strung;
A brand-new year
    Has just begun.
Shall I be brave
    And charge ahead?
With wild abandon
    Choose my thread?

The Master Weaver's
    Still small voice
Says, "You are mine.
    Mine is the choice."
In penitence
    I bow my head
And let the Master
    Choose the thread.
        —*Ethel V. Leffel*

Almost Morning

The night will soon be ended,
    The darkness gone at last.
The morning light will soon appear,
    The evening will be past.

The time you least expect it
    Is the time He will appear.
With morning sun or when day is done—
    Jesus will soon be here.

Forget about the strain of life;
    Just concentrate on when.
Trials will cease; all will be peace
    When Jesus comes again!
        —*Gean D. Smith*

Trifles

Little sparks can make great fires,
Little bricks can build great spires;
Stained-glass windows much surpass
Any made of just plain glass;
They are fragments, some quite small,
Pieced together—that is all.
Music for the world to sing
Can be played on just one string.
It's the trifles we must watch, you see,
We're weaving for eternity.
        —*Helen Kitchell Evans*

Song of Sweetness

Once I heard a song of sweetness
    As it cleft the morning air,
Sounding out its blest completeness
    Like a tender, pleading prayer.

And I sought to find the singer
    Whence the wondrous song was borne,
And I found a bird sore wounded,
    Pinioned by a cruel thorn.

I have seen a soul in sadness
    While its wings with pain were furled
Giving hope and cheer and gladness
    That should bless a weeping world.

And I knew that song of sweetness
    Was of pain and sorrow born,
And a stricken soul was singing
    With its heart against a thorn!

We are told of cruel scourging—
    Of a Savior bearing scorn—
How He died for your salvation
    With His brow against a thorn.

Ye are not above the Master!
    Will you breathe a sweet refrain?
Then His grace will be sufficient
    When your heart is pierced with pain!
        —*Jim Gibbs*

Monthly Program Material

"School Days"

Program ideas for September based on Andrew Murray's book, *With Christ in the School of Prayer.*

By Evelyn Stenbock

INTRODUCTORY THOUGHTS—
We are never too old to go back to school. Perhaps you've been thinking about it, but haven't decided what subject to study. Here's an idea: How about entering "The School of Prayer"?

SUGGESTED SONGS—
"Sweet Hour of Prayer"
"Tell It to Jesus"
"Did You Think to Pray?"
"Blessed Hour of Prayer"
"A Child of the King"
"The Beautiful Garden of Prayer"

INTRODUCING THE PRAYER BOX—
Many people have a prayer notebook in which they record prayer requests, praise items, and answers to prayer. We would like to introduce the "Prayer Box." You can begin with any small box, 3 x 5 or 4 x 6. A shoe box or recipe card file is ideal. To begin with you might bind your cards with an elastic band or ribbon, obtaining a box when you need it.

The advantage of a box is its flexibility. You will need three sections: *Prayer Needs, Answers to Prayer and Praise Items,* and *Completed.* Cards will be moved from one section to the other as prayers are answered. Cards in the *Completed* file should be kept as a reminder to you of God's faithfulness. When discouraged, you can eventually thumb through a stack of cards which will remind you of previous answers to prayer.

To begin, obtain blank file cards *(the leader may have some to give to group members for a beginning).* On each card write a prayer request: the name of a loved one, friend, or acquaintance needing prayer; prayer needs of your church or women's group; family or personal requests. As you can, obtain prayer cards from missionaries you are interested in, and file them in your box. Christmas card pictures make dandy prayer reminders. Clip them off the printed letter or cut the Christmas card to fit your box. Snapshots, school pictures, clippings from the newspaper or newsletters are all good prayer reminders. They can be pasted on the cards, or filed.

As you approach your prayer time, flip through the cards. As prayers are answered, move them to the praise section; when you hear of a prayer need, add it to your cards; once the matter is settled, make a note of final praise items on the card and file it in the *Completed* section.

TO GET ACQUAINTED—
You may wish to have each member of your group bring a photo to this meeting, or provide a photographer with a Polaroid camera to take a picture of each person present. These can be given out the first meeting, one to each person wanting to participate, and exchanged the following month. As you pray for the person whose photo you have for the month, you should make an effort to get acquainted through phone calls, visits, and friendly gestures.

The leader may choose to provide prayer cards from a missionary each month, introducing the missionary and his work before passing out the cards. Each person should be given a photo of the pastor and family if possible.

At the next meeting, and again at the final meeting of the year, ask for testimonies pertaining to the use of Prayer Boxes.

PREPARING FOR PRAYER—
As you prepare to lead your group into a meaningful prayer time, think your way through the congregation or community. You can mention shut-ins, the bereaved, the terminally ill and their loved ones, people out of work, students who are away at college, etc. Avoid making too long a list. Seek to present priority needs.

Encourage the group to record the prayer requests for their Prayer Box. If you plan to distribute photos of your pastor or missionaries, this would be a good time to do it.

DEVOTIONAL THOUGHTS—"The School of Prayer"
(This can be read, or your speaker may glean ideas from it to go along with your theme.)

From an African village comes a striking illustration about prayer. According to legend, each Christian in the village crept away from the activity surrounding the huts every day to pray. As time passed, paths appeared in the grass, marking out the sacred spots, so if one neglected his quiet time very long, the grass growing over his path made his slothfulness in prayer obvious to others. Someone would finally go to the wayward one and say, "Brother, we notice the grass is growing on the path to your place of prayer."

Sometimes we need an admonition like that. Though grass doesn't grow over our path to prayer, our neglect may become apparent in other ways. Perhaps most importantly, those who are counting on our prayer support will find their effectiveness in ministry weakened, or their daily perseverance in the faith a more difficult struggle. When we say, "Brother/Sister, I'll be praying for you," we'd better do it.

Andrew Murray, a Dutch Reformed minister of the early 1900s, was much in demand as a speaker both in Europe and South Africa. Many of his sermons were translated into English, and are available to us today. From his book *With Christ in the School of Prayer* we glean these few thoughts:

1. **Enroll in the Lord's special course of teaching in prayer.** We do this by praying, "Lord, teach me to pray." It is interesting, in light of the above illustration, that Luke 11:1 tells us Jesus was praying "in a certain place" (NIV) when His disciples asked Him about prayer. While we can pray in any place, at any time, to become real prayer warriors we need to find a quiet place, stop our busy activity, and ask the Lord to teach us. Matthew 6:6 mentions a "secret" place—a solitary spot where you can be alone with God.

2. **Realize that you are a child, and have a child's liberty of access.** Andrew Murray further points out that "the revelation of the Father gives confidence in prayer." Drawing from "The Lord's Prayer" (Matthew 6:9-13), he says, "The knowledge of God's Father-love is the first and simplest, but also the last and highest lesson in the school of prayer. . . . To appreciate this word of adoration, remember that none of the saints had in Scripture ever ventured to address God as Father!" And, he adds, "The secret of effectual prayer is to have the heart filled with the Father-love of God. . . . Our unchildlike distance from the Father hinders the answer to prayer."

    Do you know God as your Heavenly Father? Do you talk to Him throughout the day, sharing happy events, murmuring gratitude, or breathing quick prayers for help, patience, wisdom, or strength? Add to this the special time of closeting yourself to really learn to pray. As a father, God will delight in meeting you there.

    Murray goes on to say, "It is one of the terrible marks of the diseased state of the Christian life in these days that there are so many who rest content without the distinct experience of answer to prayer. . . . It is the will of God, the rule of the Father's family: every childlike, believing petition is granted. If it is not, there must be something in the prayer that is not as God would have it. Live as a child of God; then you will be able to pray as a child, and as a child you will most assuredly be heard."

    Going back to "The Lord's Prayer" a moment, the order of requests is significant. It is first *Thy* name, *Thy* kingdom, *Thy* will. Then follows give *us*, forgive *us*, lead *us*, and deliver *us*.

3. **Make prayer definite.** As an illustration, Andrew Murray refers to Mark 10: 46-51—the account of the blind man who received his sight. The blind man first cries out for mercy, but Jesus requires more of him than that, even though it is obvious what the man needs and wants. Jesus says, "What wilt thou that I should do unto thee?" The blind man gets very definite, saying simply: "I want to see!" (NIV).

    Says Murray, "Until he speaks out, he is not healed.

    "Being definite in prayer helps us to wait for the special answer and to mark it when it comes. There is a prayer in which, in everything, we make known our requests with prayer and supplications, and the reward is the sweet peace of God keeping the heart and mind. This is the prayer of trust . . . Elijah knew for certain that rain would come; God had promised it; and yet he had to pray seven times. Faith says most confidently, 'I have received it.' Patience perseveres in prayer until the gift bestowed in heaven is received on earth."

    A good lesson for us to learn—making prayer definite. For when we do, we can watch for the answer, gently reminding the Lord of our request each time we see Him if need be, trusting Him to give us the answer in His good time. And, as Andrew Murray puts it, "to mark it when it comes."

4. **"When ye stand praying, forgive."** Of all the lessons on prayer—and if you sincerely enter "Christ's School of Prayer" you will find there are many lessons—this one is possibly the hardest, as well as being the most important. Says Murray: "It is as if the Lord had learned during His life at Nazareth and afterwards that disobedience to the law of love to man was the great sin even of praying people, and the great cause of the failures of their prayer. Scripture says, 'Forgive one another even as God also in Christ forgave you.' God's full and free forgiveness is to be the rule. . . . Pardon opens the door to all God's love and blessing. When God's forgiving love has taken possession of the heart, we pray in faith, but also, we live in love. We forgive as He forgives. We seek to possess a godlike disposition; to be kept from a sense of wounded humor; from a desire to maintain our rights or to give the offender what he deserves.

"Our forgiving love to men is the condition of the prayer of faith. Unloving thoughts and words I allow to pass unnoticed throughout the day can hinder my prayer."

Well, these are just a few of the lessons that once came from the lips of a godly preacher who spoke the Dutch language in a faraway country—lessons on learning to pray, on getting to know God so well we find it easy and natural to pray, and lessons on how to remove hinderances that keep our prayer from being answered. The lessons are as relevant today, in our language, in our community— in our homes and for our hearts as they were back then. The good news is that Christ's School of Prayer is still open. And you and I can enroll!

CLOSING PRAYER—
Dear Lord, we have seen today the importance of prayer, and our hearts do respond, for we want to learn how to pray effectively. As we bow before You in a moment of silent prayer, help each of us to examine our own heart, to allow You to remove all hinderances, and then, dear Lord, enroll us in Your School of Prayer! In the name of Jesus our Savior, Amen.

PROMOTIONAL IDEAS—
For the bulletin board, a large red apple with green stem and leaf, cut from felt or red poster board, with photos, prayer cards, and the "School Days" theme to catch attention, as well as date, time, and location of meeting.

REFRESHMENTS—
Apple cider and donuts, with a bowl of polished red apples for those who may be watching their weight.

Another Year

A monologue for a New Year's meeting

By Ethel V. Leffel

New Year's Day! The year past gone into oblivion. What does New Year's mean to you? What does it mean to me?

Let's pretend that you're my next-door neighbor and I've invited you in for a cup of coffee. And maybe we'll have a cinnamon crisp that I've just taken out of the oven!

You open the door.

"Happy New Year," you say.

"Happy New Year to you, too," I greet you.

As we're visiting over coffee, we have a serious thought. "What does New Year's mean to you? What does it mean to me?" I ask.

We're still for a few minutes—not the awkward kind of silence that follows a greeting from someone on the street you haven't seen in a long time. This is a friend-to-friend kind of quietness where each respects the other's thoughts.

You break the silence.

"The New Year is like a newly plowed field on the prairie," you say. I can tell you're a South Dakota girl. I think of those beautiful, black plowed fields we had seen on a trip out west. They wouldn't stay that way for long. If they were left untended, they would soon be full of weeds. That wasn't the farmer's intention when he plowed up the land. He planned to fill it with winter wheat that would come up like a velvet carpet and wave in the summer wind bright gold and beautiful. He planned it. That was his secret.

"So teach us to number our days so that we may apply our hearts to wisdom," I quote.

I go on musing about the year: "A day is a precious commodity. A whole year is a whole bundle of precious commodities. It shouldn't be squandered aimlessly. Every day of the year is a special gift from God. He controls the months, the season, the years."

". . . And God gives us squatters' rights," you say. (South Dakota again!) You continue. "If we're Christians, our time is part of our stewardship. It isn't really our own. It belongs to God. We are responsible to Him for the way we use each day."

Another moment of silence.

I'm a flower enthusiast. Our yard has flowerbeds everywhere. Flowers of every texture, color, and form. I relate better to flowerbeds than to wide-open prairies.

The year will be many hued. Of that we may be sure! There will be births and deaths; marriages and reunions, and partings. There will be sunshine and rain. This we can count on.

There are so many weeds in the flowerbeds, if I didn't pull them constantly they would soon take over completely. Like our lives. But God made the weeds, too, probably to remind us that life isn't always a bed of roses. We have lots of weeds to pull, and we'd better pull them.

"So, friend," I say at last, "there will be good and bad. There will be glad and sad."

"But there will always be God," you, my beloved friend, say. You're always so wise. You go on: "God! There when we wake up in the morning, and when we drop wearily into bed at night."

"God! Always God!" I think. God for each moment of every day all year long.

This is what the New Year means to you and me. Isn't it a comfort to meet the New Year with no one less than God himself in charge of the rising and setting of the sun!

I'm glad there's always God!

On the Subject of Hearts

A devotional reading for Valentine's Day

By Ethel V. Leffel

Every person you meet on the busy streets of life has a heart pumping life into his body. Pumping! Pumping! Pumping! Pumping away the seconds, the minutes, the hours, the years that make up a life.

God is monitoring every beat.

A heart is a miracle of God. This miracle of God isn't black or white. It isn't Chinese, or Swedish, or Jewish. It isn't copper or fair. Hearts are all one color. Ask the doctor who specializes in open-heart surgery.

God is no respecter of persons. He doesn't care if the home is a hovel or a hacienda. He doesn't care if clothes are Paris or bargain basement, dirty or clean. God can meet man in any circumstance, in many ways, and in any place on the globe.

But you can be sure of one thing. "Man looks on the outward appearance, but God looks on the heart."

God sees a whole world of hearts. God loves the world. He doesn't love the sin and disobedience that is growing more gross every day, but He does love His creation—and His creatures.

The commandment that Jesus gave was: "Thou shalt love the Lord thy God with all thy heart, and with all thy soul, and with all thy mind." God made our hearts capable of love. He doesn't force us to love Him, though. He lets us choose to do so.

The Book of Proverbs says: "The wise in heart shall receive commandments." In Romans we read, "With the heart man believeth unto righteousness."

The Bible speaks of hearts over and over again. It speaks of melting hearts, understanding hearts, melodious hearts, and pure hearts. It also speaks of double hearts, proud hearts, unbelieving hearts, adamant hearts, stony hearts, and hearts that are not right with God.

A heart out of tune with God, a heart adamant to God's love, a heart that "would not"—this is what made Jesus weep over Jerusalem.

If Jesus wept over lost hearts then, is He doing less now?

"If they had only known," the Bible says, "they would not have crucified the Lord of glory."

Known what?

If they had only known God's great measure of love that sent Jesus to earth to die for our sins.

Have you ever hurt in your heart when you did a loving deed and the one you tried to please either ignored the gift, or rejected it?

God's great love-gift to us was the giving of His own Son, whom He loved with a love only God can possess. If your heart can hurt when love is refused, just think how God—who is capable of intense emotions—must hurt at our rejection of His gift.

The Psalmist says (Psalm 139:23-24): "Search me, O God, and know my heart: try me, and know my thoughts: And see if there be any wicked way in me, and lead me in the way everlasting." We read in Psalm 34:18, "The Lord is nigh unto them that are of a broken heart; and saveth such as be of a contrite spirit." Second Thessalonians 3:5 promises us, "And the Lord direct your hearts into the love of God, and into the patient waiting for Christ."

Jesus is coming again. With the conditions shaping up in the world as they are, that time might be sooner than we think.

God is still in the business of looking at hearts. Listen to this warning. It is a warning that could have been written for this very day in which we live. The passage, found in Luke 21:34, says: "Take heed to yourselves, lest at any time your hearts be overcharged with surfeiting, and drunkenness, and cares of this life, and so that day come upon you unawares."

You see, the surfeiting—overindulging—is a very commonplace thing, whether it be food, sports, your work, your home, your cars. It might be worse: sex, drugs, unfaithfulness to your mate. Or it might be your legitimate job. It might be anything that drives the thought of God out of your mind. This could apply to a person who has never met Christ, but it might also be directed to Christians who are not "seeking first the kingdom of God."

God wants the whole heart. He wants changed hearts. He wants pure hearts. Jesus said in the Sermon on the Mount (Matthew 5:8): "Blessed are the pure in heart, for they shall see God."

Songwriter Elisha A. Hoffman asks the piercing question:

> Is thy heart right with God?
> Wash'd in the crimson flood,
> Cleansed and made holy, humble and lowly,
> Right in the sight of God?

Remember, God looks at hearts!

King of Glory Easter Program

(Outline for a complete program including luncheon, special numbers, and speaker.)

By Carolyn R. Scheidies

DECORATIONS—For each table, a large white cross surrounded by lilies. Small plastic lilies can be fastened to nut cups. A banner over head table quotes John 11:25.

MENU—
Triumphal Entry—*Beverage*
Welcoming Palms—*Tossed Salad*
Surging Crowds—*Peas*
Heaven's Lamb—*Meat*
Shining Clouds—*Mashed Potatoes with butter*
Stones Away—*Rolls*
Hallelujah Chorus—*Desert*

PROGRAM—
Invocation
Dinner
Song—"Low in the Grave He Lay"
Choral Groups—Scripture Reading from Psalm 24
  (Three groups, or three people, position themselves in a triangle: A ^{B} C.)

GROUP A—The earth is the Lord's, and the fulness thereof; the world, and they that dwell therein.

GROUP B—For he hath founded it upon the seas, and established it upon the floods.

GROUP C—Who shall ascend into the hill of the Lord? or who shall stand in his holy place?

GROUP A—He that hath clean hands, and a pure heart; who hath not lifted up his soul unto vanity, nor sworn deceitfully.

GROUP B—He shall receive the blessing from the Lord, and righteousness from the God of his salvation.

ALL GROUPS—This is the generation of them that seek him, that seek thy face, O Jacob. Selah.

Group A—Lift up your heads, O ye gates; and be ye lifted up, ye everlasting doors; and the King of glory shall come in.

Group C—Who is this King of glory?

Group A—The Lord, strong and mighty,

Group B—The Lord, mighty in battle.

Group A—Lift up your heads, O ye gates: even left them up, ye everlasting doors; and the King of glory shall come in.

Group C—Who is this King of glory?

All Groups—The Lord of hosts, he is the King of glory. Selah.

Solo—"Open the Gates of the Temple" or "I Know That My Redeemer Liveth"

Narrator—"I am the resurrection and the life: he that believeth in me, though he were dead, yet shall he live" (John 11:25).

Speaker or Easter Film

Song—"Christ, the Lord, Is Risen Today"

The Covered Dish Convention

(A Luncheon Program)

By Gail Blanton

This devotion is designed to be used at any covered dish dinner meeting. However, this program will differ from most schedules in that it will be presented before dinner. This should be a well-kept secret. Have the dishes placed on the tables as usual, pretending the dinner is about to begin. Ask everyone to be seated and socialize while waiting for final preparations. When it is time for the program, the hostess may have to ask many who are still standing to be seated. You should alert anyone who must for medical reasons eat on a regular schedule, as well as the ladies who will place the ice in the glasses. Everyone else should be totally surprised, very hungry, and somewhat impatient as the program is presented—which is exactly the effect you want to produce. To begin, the hostess should announce that we have a local television crew with us today who are filming the meeting. Announcer should come immediately holding a microphone and pretending to be talking into a camera.

ANNOUNCER—Good afternoon *(evening)*, ladies and gentlemen. This is Corning Ware coming to you from the annual Covered Dish Convention in Pyrex. Activities have been in full swing for the past two days with none of the misconduct that plagued the convention last year. All dishes have kept themselves discreetly covered and thus far none have been tabled. I now stand in the famed Casserole Hall, where the highlight of the convention is about to begin—the grand finale known as the Blue Ribbon Banquet. In this event each recipient of a blue ribbon will display his or her winning dish and speak a few words about its characteristics. Let's join the ceremonies now.

(The winners approach one at a time. If they do not wish to memorize the verse, they may carry an empty covered dish, raise the lid, and read the verse.)

WINNER 1—Hi, I'm Psalm 34:8, and my dish was chosen the winner in the appetizer division: "O taste and see that the Lord is good" (KJV).

WINNER 2—Hello. I received first prize in the Practicality Competition. I'm Isaiah 43:2 and my dish was chosen because it is heat-proof and can be totally immersed in water without hurting its quality. "When you pass through the waters I will be with you; and through the rivers, they shall not overwhelm you; when you walk through fire you shall not be burned and the flame shall not consume you" (RSV).

WINNER 3—Hi. I'm Galatians 5:22 and my fruit salad was a winner. "The fruit of the Spirit is love, joy, peace, patience, kindness, goodness, faithfulness, gentleness, self-control" (RSV).

WINNER 4—Good afternoon. I'm Matthew 25:35, and my dish was the favorite of the Benevolence Committee. "I was hungry and you gave me food" (RSV).

WINNER 5—Hello. I'm Matthew 5:6 and my dish was chosen as the most satisfying and filling. "Blessed are those who hunger and thirst for righteousness, for they shall be satisfied" (RSV).

WINNER 6—Hi. I'm Matthew 16:6 and my dish took the distinguished award of the AHA—Association of Hypocrite Avoidance—because its ingredients provide strong preventive medicine. "Take heed and beware of the leaven of the Pharisees and Sadducees" (RSV).

(Winners 7 and 8 approach together.)

WINNER 7—A tie was declared in the Health Food Division. I'm Matthew 5:13 and my dish was chosen for its appeal to those on restricted diets. It requires no salt. "You are the salt of the earth" (RSV).

WINNER 8—And I'm Matthew 7:16. My dish was selected because of its unique contribution to psychological health. "You will know them by their fruits" (RSV).

WINNER 9—Hi. I'm John 4:14, the winner in the Beverage Division. "Whoever drinks of the water that I shall give him will never thirst" (RSV).

WINNER 10—Good afternoon. 1 Peter 2:2 here. The Commission on Reborn Infants has chosen my dish because of its large quantity of milk. "Like newborn babes, long for the pure spiritual milk, that by it you may grow up to salvation" (RSV).

ANNOUNCER—Ladies and gentlemen, if you'll pay close attention now, you are about to see the most exciting part of this convention—the presentation of the grand prize winner. Yes, there she is. You can see her now. And the crowd here in Casserole Hall is going wild as she approaches the stage. As the cheering dies down, let's listen now so we don't miss a word of this memorable speech.

WINNER 11—Thank you. I'm Isaiah 55:1 and the judges have concluded that my dish has the most desirable quality of all—it is absolutely free. "Ho, every one who thirsts, come to the waters; and he who has no money, come, buy and eat! Come, buy wine and milk without money and without price" (RSV).

ANNOUNCER—Well, that concludes our ceremonies today, brought to you live from these famous surroundings, whose own founder said, "Even . . . the Son of man came not to be served, but to serve" (Matthew 20:28, RSV). And remember, all of these winning recipes plus many more are featured in this wonderful recipe book *(hold up a Bible)*, available in any store or by writing this station. This is Corning Ware saying so long, and be sure you are using this authentic recipe book, whose outstanding author has declared, "He who believes in me shall never hunger."

HOSTESS—The usual procedure at a dinner such as this is to have the shortest prayer and the longest reach possible, rush right in and eat to your heart's content, or your heart's burn as the case may be, and then settle back to squirm, sigh, or snore your way through the devotion. Is it possible we have things backward? Isn't that the way it is all too often in our lives? We are so aware of our physical appetites that we can't wait to satisfy them. What's more, we enjoy the process. By now, no doubt, you are feeling the urgent demands of that physical craving that has been kept waiting. How strong is your spiritual hunger? When was the last time you caught yourself rushing to satisfy some tremendous craving in your spiritual appetite? Today—for this one dinner—for this one hour—we have fed our spiritual selves before we fed our physical selves. For the Christian, it is simply a matter of good taste.

A One-Act Play

Del's Woodsman

A one-act play for three women

By Ted Scoggins

SETTING—
A nursing home. Three rocking chairs.

CHARACTERS—
Narrator

Delcenia—An elderly lady, carrying a Bible. Her speech is moderate and direct. One senses a certain strength and wisdom about her.

Ann—A thin, fragile person, slow of speech and at times living in her own little world, losing touch with reality.

Birdie—Heavy and not as neatly dressed as other ladies. Such things are not important to her. She speaks quickly and has a slight air of coldness—mentally quick, but lacking wisdom and compassion to balance her sharp tongue.

As the play begins, Ann sits in the middle chair, quietly knitting. Birdie sits in one of the other chairs, rocking and staring ahead. Narrator walks to stage and begins his story.

Narrator—There was once a lady—an elderly lady she was, and a very sweet and gentle one, at that. She used to tell an enchanting tale about a magnificent woodsman. Once she was asked for the origin of the story. She confessed that she simply made the story up. The story simply popped up one day during a devotional meeting. You see, at that time, she was living in a nursing home. Each day, she and two of her friends got together and had a little devotional meeting. This is the story she told.

(The narrator turns and motions with his outstretched arm toward the two ladies in the rocking chairs behind him. He then exits the stage and after a moment, Delcenia enters with her Bible in hand and the story begins.)

Ann—Well, Delcenia, we thought you were going to forget us today.

Delcenia—I was just reading a nice lengthy letter from my son and his wife and children.

Birdie—What's wrong with them? My boy won't write me unless something's wrong.

Delcenia—Oh, no, nothing is wrong. They just wanted to write to me.

Ann—Are they coming for a visit?

Delcenia—They didn't say. They'll come when they can.

Ann—That's the way my children are, too, Delcenia. It's "when we can" and "pretty soon" and, oh, sometimes I think they would be pleased to be without the trouble of coming to visit at all.

Delcania—Now, Ann, you're exaggerating.

Birdie—I don't think she is, Del. Why, my boy and that sorry bunch he runs with—they load up their boat and run to the lake without a second thought that I might be wishing for a visit.

Ann—Well, my children are not that bad.

Delcenia—Birdie, do you ever write your son?

Birdie—Now, Del, you, of all people, should know it costs money to write. He's got the money. Let him write me.

Ann—If he's like my children, he doesn't want you involved in his business, anyway.

Birdie—Well, thank the good Lord, he's nothing like your children, and anyway, I don't insist on knowing his every move the way you do with yours, Ann.

Ann—I don't *insist* on anything from them. They don't tell me anything they don't want me to know.

Birdie—You bother and pry so much until they tell you everything just to get you to hush.

Ann—I do no such thing, Birdie! Why I . . .

Delcenia *(interrupts)*—Ladies! Gracious ladies, please. I think it's time we begin our daily devotional. *(She opens her Bible.)* Ann, would you like to lead us in a prayer as we begin!

Ann—I feel sick. *(She begins to stare straight ahead and does not appear to hear the several subsequent lines between Birdie and Delcenia.)*

Birdie—I'm in no praying mood, either.

Delcenia—What's the matter with you two today?

Birdie—Nothing's the matter with me—it's—it's just—

Delcenia—Just what?

Birdie—It's just—it's just that sometimes I get tired of being an old woman. Do you know what I mean, Del?

Delcenia—Well, maybe you could explain.

Birdie—Oh, it has to do with feeling useless, I think, Del. It just seems futile for us to keep going when we're accomplishing nothing—getting nothing done. What's the use? Our time has come and gone, Del. We're just . . .

Ann *(jumps up, interrupting suddenly and loudly, looking frantic and terrified)*—I'm going to die! Oh, I'm going to die! Oh, I'm going to die! Oh, help meeee! Oh, I'm going to die!

(Birdie and Delcenia, looking startled, try to restrain Ann. Ann pushes their arms away, never ceasing to carry on with "I'm going to die!")

Birdie *(loudly in order to be heard above Ann)*—She's hysterical!

Delcenia *(loudly)*—Let's see if we can get her to sit down.

Birdie—Hush, Ann! Do you want them to come and drag you off to the hospital?

(Delcenia, at last, pats Ann on the cheek. Ann stops shouting and bursts into tears, then Birdie places Ann back into her chair. Ann continues sobbing. Birdie stands aside and Delcenia kneels beside Ann, holding Ann's hands in comfort. After several moments, Ann's sobbing reduces to sniffles.)

Delcenia—What's wrong, Ann? What's the matter?

Ann *(sniffling)*—I'm going to die.

Birdie—Don't tell me you've just now figured *that* out.

Delcenia—Well, talk to us about it, Ann. We're your friends. Tell us what's bothering you, honey.

Ann—I don't know if I can.

Delcenia—Sure you can. Just say what's on your heart.

Ann *(sniffling slightly and beginning to regain composure)*—I'm sorry I made such an outburst. Please forgive me.

Delcenia—That's perfectly alright, honey. You don't have to apologize to us.

Ann—Thank you—that's sweet of you.

Delcenia—Now, let's talk about it.

Ann—Oh, it just hit me, Delcenia. It was death—as dark and black and ugly as you could ever imagine. It just hit me—there is no way I can escape it. It's coming. It's going to get me.

Delcenia—Everyone will die, honey. You've always known that.

Ann—I know, but—but you two sit down now. I'm alright. *(They return to their chairs.)* It's been building up all day. You see, I've been—I've been thinking about my late husband, and about the children, and about all the plans we had a long time ago. As I look back, Del, I see that nothing—not one thing—

worked out like we planned. Oh, we wanted a big house in the country and a swimming pool and a greenhouse. We wanted a place where we could enjoy watching the kids grow up. And we wanted the kids to all go off to college, then come back and build their houses on our land beside us. We all could have our evening meals together, at my table, and I would be such a gracious hostess . . .

Birdie—Such dreams!

Ann—But look how it turned out. My husband died and left me all alone. He just laid down and died! We never even got our house. My oldest son dropped out of school and married a girl way below our social level. She was his downfall, too. She made him work in the factory. My other son married a sweet girl—a good school teacher—but they are so busy. A boring, dumb old lady like me can't compete with the exciting life they lead.

Birdie—Your daughter did very well.

Ann—Yes, but Mrs. College Professor lives so far away with that foreigner husband of hers. Here I am! Oh, how I do love sitting here in this chair, knowing that the sun will come up tomorrow. But I saw myself lying cold and very dead inside a sealed coffin. The thought of my death just suddenly overwhelmed me. I've always been able to put it out of my mind, but this time it won't go. It's presence is so awful! It has cornered me and I am trapped, Del. There is no relief from it.

Birdie—Oh, that's silly.

Ann—It's not silly to me, Birdie.

Birdie—Well, it's silly to me. Silly! Just silly! And ridiculous!

Delcenia—Why is it silly, Birdie?

Birdie—She says there is no relief from death. It's *life* that there is no relief from! There is nothing, and I mean nothing, in this world but sin, pain, and heartache! Everytime a person tries to do something good, it turns out wrong! Everything a person works hard to build up gets torn to pieces in an instant! Every special loved one is taken from you! You can count only on heartache! It is the one thing you can count on! So death itself is relief! Relief from this stupid, useless world and all its false hope and trouble! You're silly to fear it, Ann. I welcome death! I long for it! I—I—(*she shakes her head in disgust, crosses her arms, and turns her head away from the other two ladies. After a moment, Delcenia rises slowly from her chair and walks slowly to near the front corner of the stage. She stops, facing away from the other ladies and with Bible in hand, she looks upward thoughtfully for a long moment before she speaks. The script can be placed in the open Bible for referrel.*)

Delcenia—My two dear friends, if you will, please imagine this. Imagine that you found yourself walking in a beautiful wood. Yes, a beautiful wood. The sun is radiant, and peeps through the trees, and the breeze just kisses you right on the face. And you are filled with joy at being in such a place. You are free to run through these woods and enjoy them until you are overflowing. Such a lovely place!

Then you come to a fence with a sign that reads "Do not cross beyond." You are free. You decide that your wisdom must be greater than the wisdom which placed the sign there. Therefore, you cross the fence and run into the forest beyond. The woods grow very deep and very dark. You soon realize you have lost your way and there seems to be no hope for you. So, you sit down, in the darkness, against a tree, hang your head and weep.

But then a gentle hand, yes, a firm but gentle hand reaches out to you. You accept that hand and you are lifted up! *(She turns around and looks back toward Birdie and Ann.)* That hand is the hand of a strong, kind woodsman. You look into His eyes and He says simply, "Follow Me." So you follow Him, and along your way He tells you wonderful stories, and He teaches with such wisdom that everything begins to take on meaning and you begin to see with a new vision. Oh, He is such a magnificent, splendid woodsman.

(She walks slowly to the opposite side of the stage, looking away from the other ladies as she continues her story.)

After a while, He leads you to a narrow trail, and He tells you to follow that trail, for it will lead you to a new and even grander forest than the one you once ran free in. He says He will be waiting for you at the end of the trail, but first He must go back into the dark woods. He has tears in His eyes. You ask what is the matter and He says He will pay the penalty for your trespassing in the dark woods, He turns and disappears into the darkness. How troubled you feel, yet you obey.

You begin the journey along the narrow trail. On the third day of your journey, as you sit resting, you feel a gentle touch, and you turn quickly to see the face of the kind woodsman. His face is aglow and He tells you that the penalty is paid. He says He must go on to the grand new forest to prepare for you, and He also says that once you have followed the narrow trail to rejoin Him there, the dark woods will be burned and destroyed forever. Then, the woodsman is gone again. *(She turns and looks at Ann and Birdie.)*

You long to rejoin Him, just as He longs to rejoin you. And so you continue on that narrow trail—that long, dark, and narrow trail—sustained only by the hope of being rejoined with that magnificent Woodsman. Ladies, do you hear my story? Do you know this Woodsman of whom I speak?

Birdie—Well, sure, it's a clever little story, Del. But it seems to have little to say to me.

Delcenia—Oh, but it does, Birdie. If you come near to the end of that narrow trail, as we certainly have, and you are able to look back and see no purpose in it—if it's only the troubles and hardships along the way that you see—then the reason for having a trail at all has been lost to you and you've surely forgotten your Woodsman. That is, and I'm sorry to say this, assuming you ever even reached out and accepted His hand in the first place!

Ann—It was a good story, Delcenia.

Delcenia—What good did you see in it, Ann?

Ann—Well, it had a good ending.

Delcenia—But for you—what does it mean for you?

Ann—I don't know that it means anything specifically for me.

Delcenia—Well, Ann, allow me to be frank with you. I am your friend or else I would not say this. You also lose sight of your Woodsman. You build campfires and shelters along the narrow trail, then when the time comes to move along, you don't want to douse out the fire and take up the tent. You want to cling to these small comforts along the trail. You forget the greatest comfort—that of being rejoined with the Woodsman.

We are on the trail of the Living God. He is our Woodsman. The hope of being reunited with Jesus—that is what sustains us. Jesus himself will meet us at the end of our narrow trail!

Ann—But why do I have to die!

Delcenia—When does death come, Ann? Did it not come when you reached out and accepted the hand of the Woodsman? Did you not give up the way that got you lost? And did you not gain the Woodsman?

Birdie—You're talking crazy, Del.

Delcenia *(she raises her hands in expression)*—Well, if what I'm saying is crazy, then I'm long gone!

Ann—Oh, my!

Delcenia—When this old body dies, it will be just a passage for me! Do you understand that, ladies? Just a passage! *(She opens her Bible and reads 1 Corinthians 15:55-58. They pause in silence for a moment. Delcenia holds her Bible open, savoring the words.)*

Birdie—Come and sit beside us.

(Delcenia moves the chair and sits gently.)

Delcenia—Do you see, Birdie, that our time has not come and gone. Yes, I know that we are not as active as we once were. We don't do as much as we used to do. But—but I think ours is not a time for doing. It is a time for being. All our lives our Lord has been shaping us—molding us—making us into a person like we never imagined we'd be. All those accomplishments and all that activity were a part of His work, but they also were a part of His making us into His persons. Now it's time for us to be His persons. Those young active ones will notice, I think.

And, Ann, you know that all our lives our Lord has required us to renounce this world, to give it up completely, so that we might gain life. And for us, the only life, the only real comfort, the only fulfillment, is in being with Him.

So, ladies, I know it is hard along the way. I know it is. But we have His Word, and I believe we even have little bits and little tastes of heaven while we're here.

Birdie—I'd like to hear an example.

Delcenia—We have one another. That closeness we have. It must be a little taste of heaven, don't you think?

Ann—I think so. And you know, it's all so amazing to me.

(Birdie smiles, jumps up from her chair, takes the object Ann has been knitting and puts it on her own head, takes Delcenia's Bible, then begins waving her arm

in time, pretending to lead an imaginary chorus as she begins singing "Amazing Grace." Halfway through the first verse, Delcenia and Ann join her. Together they joyously sing the entire hymn. When they finish, they all laugh and Birdie hands back the knitted object and the Bible, then she sits back down and reaches across and takes Ann's hand in hers.)

Birdie—I do truly love you both, my dear friends.

(Delcenia takes Ann's other hand.)

Ann *(lifts their joined hands upward)*—Praise to the good Lord who brought three such fine ladies together.

(They hold up their joined hands for a moment, then let them down, and each lady returns to her individual activity. Delcenia reads her Bible silently; Ann continues knitting; Birdie just rocks in her rocking chair. The narrator walks casually back to front-center stage.)

Narrator—Well, that's pretty much the story, except I guess I should tell you that later on that very night—later after that very devotional meeting—Ann died in her sleep.

And it might interest you to know that some few months after the time of that meeting, Birdie's son and his family came and invited her to move in with them. As far as I know, she did.

As for Delcenia—well—she continued her sweet Christian witness until the day she, too, rejoined her Woodsman.

Mother's Day Banquet

A Hawaiian Evening

Planned by Helen Kitchell Evans

INVITATION—Your daughter cordially invites you to attend a Luau
        Date... Time... Place
        Please wear a Hawaiian muumuu if possible.
        Please let us know if you plan to attend.
        Until we see you.... "ALOHA"

DECORATIONS—To have a Hawaiian atmosphere there should be flowers and greenery. If you have plenty of vines and green plants, flowers and fruit can be combined to give the appearance of abundance. Use fresh pineapples with other fresh fruits mixed in the greenery, and for centerpieces. An artificial flower here and there adds color to the greenery.

FAVORS—Small dolls with feet glued to a small white round of cardboard can be dressed in a hula skirt of green crepe paper with a little tissue paper lei.

PARTICIPANTS' COSTUMES—All taking part in the program could wear hula skirts, or just the smaller girls that might sing or recite. All participants should wear leis—more than one, as in Hawaii, if desired. Leis can be presented to all mothers as they enter or are seated, or to specially honored mothers during the program.

HOW TO MAKE HULA SKIRTS—Dye old sheets or purchase inexpensive green material. Measure the child's waist. The strip that is used to go around the waist should be long enough to go around four times. This adds to the fulness of the skirt. Measure skirt length to the ankles, the width of the wasteband, and attach by machine. From the hemline up, slit the skirt in strips of 2 to 3 inches. They will hang more like leaves if they are torn, rather than cut. Wear the skirts over leotards with swim tops or sleeveless blouses.

HOW TO MAKE LEIS—Take small pieces of tissue paper, any color, 3" x 5" or smaller, and twist in the middle to form a bow. Using a needle with a large eye and a string, thread enough bows on to make a lei of desired length.

FLOWERS—All on the program should wear a flower in their hair.

Menu—

                          Hawaiian punch
          Green onions   Carrot sticks
                          Salted Nuts
                      Tossed Green Salad
            Turbot with Vegetable Sauce Added
                     Baked Potato Ono*
    Maia† Nut Bread   Oahu‡ Fruit Cocktail

    †*Maia—banana*   *Ono-ono—delicious, tasty*   ‡*Oahu—name of island*

Recipe for Turbot with Vegetable Sauce—

        2 lbs. turbot (or halibut, haddock, or other fish)
        6 Tbsp. margarine or cooking oil
        2 tsp. salt
        1 4-oz. can sliced mushrooms
        ¼ cup chopped onion
        2 Tbsp. flour
        1½ cups milk or half and half
        1 cup defrosted peas or drained canned peas
        2 Tbsp. chopped pimento
        ¼ cup grated Parmesan cheese
        1 Tbsp. lemon juice

Directions: Thaw frozen fish. Turbot should be washed several times in cold water. Place in shallow baking dish. Cover with 2 Tbsp. melted margarine or cooking oil and sprinkle with 1 tsp. salt. Bake at 350° for 25-30 minutes, or until fish flakes easily when tested with a fork. Baste with pan juices several times during baking.

To prepare sauce (may be done day before using)—Cook mushrooms and onion in remaining 4 Tbsp. melted margarine until onion is tender. Stir in flour and remaining tsp. of salt. Add milk or half and half and cook, stirring constantly until thickened. Add peas, pimento, 2 Tbsp. parmesan cheese, and lemon juice.

Drain fish and arrange on heated serving platter. Spoon sauce over fish. Sprinkle with remaining cheese.

To determine the amount of fish to prepare, divide the number of guests by six and multiply the above recipe accordingly.

Recipe for Baked Potatoes Ono—

        3 medium baking potatoes
        ½ pint sour cream
        ½ cup finely chopped chives
        2 tsp. garlic juice
        4 large slices swiss cheese, chopped
        Salt and pepper to taste

Directions: Wash and bake potatoes for one hour or until done. Remove from oven and cut in half, scooping out the potatoes. Mash well. Add salt and pepper, sour cream, chives, and 2 slices of swiss cheese. Mix well, Place back in potato shells, sprinkle with chives, cheese, and paprika for color.

Place under broiler five minutes or if easier, rebake 30 minutes in a moderate oven. Serves 6.

RECIPE FOR MAIA NUT BREAD—

½ cup butter
1 cup sugar
2 eggs

½ cup chopped nuts
4 mashed bananas
2 cups flour
1 tsp. soda

Directions: Cream butter and sugar. Add eggs, nuts, bananas, flour, and soda. Bake in a greased pan 50-60 minutes, 350°.

OAHU FRUIT SALAD—Using whatever fresh fruits are available, cube the fruit and mix together. Do not add sugar. (Melons, grapes, bananas, pineapple, etc., should be used.)

INFORMATION ABOUT HAWAII TO BE USED BY EMCEE *(Additional information can be obtained from the library or tourist brochures.)*—Before the white man came to the islands, the fun-loving Hawaiians were enjoying "luaus"— feasts—for just about any special occasion: weddings, babies, and betrothals. Everyone helped in preparation for the feast. History records that sailors from all parts of the world were amazed at the hospitality of the Hawaiians.

Luaus can be a spur of the moment gathering or may involve days of planning. Regardless, the "aloha" spirit is always present. Today the language of Hawaii is English, but among many of the older people you will find phrases used and handed down from earlier generations.

When missionaries came to the islands, there was no written language. All their culture was transmitted through chants and songs. The Hawaiian alphabet was given to these early people by missionaries. There are only 12 letters: a, e, i, o, u, and 7 consonants: h, k, l, m, n, p, w. Every syllable of each word ends in a vowel. Pronounce "a" as "ah" (as in wash); "e" as a long a (as in day); "i" as a long e (as in me); "u" as "oo" (as in noon); "o" as long o (as in blow).

Beside your plate is a booklet with some words and phrases in it. Have fun "speaking Hawaiian" tonight!

HAWAIIAN WORDS AND PHRASES:

How are you?	Pehea oe?
I'm fine	Maika'l no wau
Thank you very much	Mahalo a nui loa
Come and eat	Mai e 'ai
Come here	Hele mai
Come in; enter	Komo mai
Happy Birthday	Hau'oli la hanau
Until we meet again	A hui hou kaua
Cat	Popoki
Child	Keiki
Rain	Ua